Contrary

Contrary

Ruth Roach Pierson

Tightrope Books

Tightrope Books
602 Markham Street
Toronto, Ontario
M6G 2L8 Canada
www.TightropeBooks.com

ONTARIO ARTS COUNCIL
CONSEIL DES ARTS DE L'ONTARIO

Edited by John Reibetanz.
Copyedited by Shirarose Wilensky.
Cover design by David Bigham.
Cover art by Rebecca Cowan.
Text design by Shirarose Wilensky.
Author photo by Sue MacLeod.

Canada Council
for the Arts

Conseil des Arts
du Canada

Produced with the support of the Canada Council for the Arts and the Ontario Arts Council.

Printed in Canada on 100% post-consumer recycled paper.

LIBRARY AND ARCHIVES CANADA CATALOGUING IN PUBLICATION

Pierson, Ruth Roach, 1938–
    Contrary / Ruth Roach Pierson.

Poems.
ISBN 978-1-926639-33-8

I. Title.

PS8581.I2815C65 2011   C811'.6   C2011-900019-9

In memory of
Father Richard R. Roach, S. J.
(1934–2008)

Table of Contents

Visiting Neruda

Dear Richard

Falling

Visiting Neruda

"I think it's, in a sense, laughable to say poetry is impersonal, because the motive is terribly personal. And if you end up writing about a cup, there is some personal reason that you're writing about that, and some personal way that you're approaching its dimension, or color, or placement in the universe. We can't hide ourselves."

Kay Ryan

Albrecht Dürer's *Adam and Eve* (1504)

Gouging, scratching the many
infinitesimally fine lines
into the copper's hard surface:
what tremendous physical effort
and endurance Dürer summoned.
Just look at the microscopic detail—
veined bark of the forest trees,
the parrot's feathers and beak,
craggy rocks and tufts of grass
off in the distance and, up close,
a mouse's tail, a serpent's scales and fangs,
fur of a cat and rabbit resting
at the feet of the first humans.
Adam's head helmeted in Greek curls,
waves of hair streaming down Eve's
back, the antlers of a goat, horns
of a cow, both peacefully inhabiting
the *Schwarzwald* garden of paradise
in the last Edenic moments before
that fateful first bite or maybe
just after Eve sampled the fruit and is
already suffering the consequences and so
begging the engraver to conceal
with a cluster of trifoliate leaves
not only her genitals but also
Adam's, who reaches down with his left arm
to receive, from Eve's hand and the snake's
maw, the proffered *Apfel*.
The branch in Adam's right arm
already raised to flagellate himself
for succumbing to the temptation

put in his path by a wily reptile
and a woman turned Jezebel. Her sloping shoulders
and rounded belly and thighs suggest,
in sharp contrast to Adam's muscled body,
a leisured life of languor and stultifying
boredom leaving her more susceptible
to curiosity than Adam, whose self-important
pre-occupation with naming all the creatures
had driven her insane for days,
desperate for a scheme
to gain and hold his attention.

Best God-Damned Poet in the USA

One spring afternoon after class
we all adjourned to the Red Robin Tavern,
and Roethke slapped me on the rump
declaring it plenty firm without the girdle.

"It wasn't in the mind of girls to write,"
Nuala O'Faolain remembers of Ireland
in the early '60s. Nor was writing in the mind
of Seattle girls in those constricted years. Poets
were like Theodore Roethke: bigger-than-life,
male, slightly unstable. Living his idea

of the Dylan Thomas life,
the wannabe poet John Pym became
a brawling, raucous frequenter of taverns.
One night, in the Blue Moon, he swept
all the bottles and pitchers to the floor, then,
losing balance, slipped and fell, suffering

a deep gash to his thigh. He walked around
pantless for days, displaying his dressed wound
like a badge. One night, bare-legged
and drunk, shirt-tail flapping like sails
in a gale-force wind, he showed up
at my apartment door. I managed
to talk him out of coming inside,

but I never managed to write, not one single
line, not for years. Though I read,
thanks to Roethke—Louise Bogan, Léonie Adams,
Denise Levertov, and, above all,

Roethke himself—the mystical, magnificent, towering Ted Roethke.

I Want to Be a Living Work of Art

Augustus John's *The Marchesa Casati* (1919)

No proper bourgeois woman would have commissioned
such a portrait, though maybe a well-kept mistress might.
How different from the studies of convalescents, orphans
and nuns Augustus's sister painted, repetitively rendering her sitters
as self-effacing, solitary figures, head and eyes
lowered over a book, at their elbow a small round table
holding an empty tea cup or china plate—sidelined

as Gwen herself must often have felt in the company
of her more famous brother, renowned for his
exuberance. Could a woman artist of her generation,
living apart from the art world and in a brother's shadow,
would she, with her meditative bent and muted, chalky palette,
have trusted herself to capture a Marchesa Luisa on canvas?

Is it her hair (flagrantly orange and unruly), her pose
(provocative and haughtily come-hither),
the gown (flounced like a negligee, and of a stuff so fine
as to be nearly transparent), or is it
her kohl-rimmed belladonna eyes, rouged
cheeks, red-painted mouth, or the way she rests
her clasped hands on her hip,
index finger crooked? Or the angle
of her head, the smoulder in that over-
the-shoulder look, elbow coquettishly cocked?

The brazen flamboyance of Augustus's Casati
startles almost a full century after she sat for her portrait
or rather stood—*souverain*, radiating serene confidence
in her flaunted sexuality, her pre-eminent entitlement.

Frederick Varley, *Lake Shore with Figure* (1922–23)

A tall slip of a woman
with a flapper's bob but lacking
the flapper's carefree air:
did he only chance upon her
stranded on the rocks
or did he follow her there?

And her dress—a long silken jumper
in a peach sheen over a blouse
of luminous turquoise, echoed
by the shimmer from an unseen sun,
rising or setting, in the cloud-strewn sky.

What did she embody for him?
Supplication? Longing? Youth?
I try to visualize her walking to the spot
in elegant shoes to match her gown.

But she's sitting back on her heels,
legs folded under torso,
arms hanging loose at her sides—
the focus on the *teinte* of her dress,
lips and cheeks.

It takes effort to pull my eyes off her
and scan the starkness of the site—
the shore lined by boulders, rounded or sheared,
her body kneeling in the concave join
of three in the foreground.

Once arrived in that austere place,
why has she sunk to her knees,
brows knitted? Overcome
with perplexed empathy
or pained rapture? Some
disaccord of thought and feeling,

a silvery aquamarine gloss
tinged with abalone iridescence
splashed across the patch of rocky shore
where the woman in peach has sunk down.

Laura Muntz Lyall's *Oriental Poppies* (ca. 1915)

As if dipped in the palette of Monet's
water lilies, these poppies float
in a wash of sunlight, but the female figure
is all Lyall, the slender body
bending forward geisha-like
with delicate fingers to pluck a bouquet
from a swirl of sleep-inducing blossoms
nodding on their spindly stems, one
curved like the neck of a Tiffany lamp,
the sweet-faced woman's tresses
a slightly deeper echo of the orange petals,
her gown bluer than the glimpses of sky,
the entire scene verging on the saccharine,
the sentimental, an opiate Arcady
Lyall conjured to forget
the red poppies of Belgium and France.

Insufficiently Consequential

She wonders was there ever a Faustian legend
where a woman enters into a pact with the devil. Not in Marlowe,
at any rate, or Goethe, Gounot, Mann. Weighed down
by insignificance and the longing to be of consequence,
she would have liked to strike such a deal, no matter the cost,
no matter where it might lead.
                                        But the fork-tongued Mephistopheles
in the flesh proved laconic as a wheat farmer, hypersensitive
to open air and daylight as a common garden mole. Negotiations
bogged down. He scorned her offer to give up writing
poems every evening before bed. She should have known
he wouldn't understand this daily practice as the gyroscope
balancing her life. Should have known he wanted nothing
less than her immortal soul.
                                        But how to bargain away
something you don't possess? She considered heaven and hell
metaphors at best, and regarded Evil's power as finite,
earth-bound. No wonder Lucifer grew bored
with her modest ambition, dismissed it as appetite devoid
of that fire in the belly which signals genius, and moved on
to more flamboyant prey, worthier of his skills at seduction and betrayal.

In her twenties, she had bristled at Louise Bogan's
"Women have no wilderness in them,"
but now she wonders.

Frederick Varley's *Dharana* (ca. 1932)

"*Dharana*, Group of Seven,"
says the curator, gesturing
at the Varley as she sweeps past,
rushing to the next piece.

Dharana—immovable concentration
of the mind, first step
in the subtle inner practice
of Samyana Yoga—is not
the name of the anorexic figure,
seated, head tilted back, wide-open eyes
gazing skyward, hands pressed
palm-down onto her thighs.

A rose-tint remnant of the Aurora borealis
brushes the mountains. Enraptured,
she breathes her relief at being alive
to witness the beginning of another day,
her back straight as a ship's
mast, uplifted face expectant,
sensuous lips parted.

The wood of the porch
where she sits is silvered
and shines like the awakened sky
heralding some revelation,
some possibility to appease,
to compensate for the daily suppression
of self she performs
in her role as the painter's
dutiful wife.

Memories of Madrid

a dancer who sang
or a singer who danced—the images
swim together in her mind

and it hardly matters

what's important is how his body
moved—back arched, agonized longing
in the curve of his raised arm, lifted
chin and sideways turn of his head

sharp staccato clack
of black heeled shoes, imperious
clap of hands

she felt in no way cheapened but rather
exalted by his naked yet
constrained display of desire
and she lusted after him

given the slightest sign
she would have raced to his side
flung herself at his feet

but the best she could do
during her two weeks in Madrid
was to finagle a seat every night
at the table closest to the stage
in the smoke-filled dimly-lit café

and picture herself his partner in the dance

Keep Away

Jeff Wall's *Double Self-Portrait* (1979)

Gänger doppelt. A-
symmetrical
mirror imaging. Left
or right—which
is the better three-
quarter profile?

Room sparingly furnished. Bucket chair
in white plastic. Chesterfield,
drab, draped in polyester blanket.
Vent near floor, door
slightly ajar. Airless
dialogue.

Only a quizzical stare—times two.
Defensive. Doubtful. Each figure
in mis/matching attire—white shirts,
one collared, one collarless, and dark pants,
one brownish, the other black. Imbalanced
duplication, backlit
and frozen in time.

This viewer eyes
the eyes. The wary ones
of the man with crossed arms say:
*keep away, my lips are sealed, I want
nothing from you.* Those of the startled man,
one hand resting on chair, the other on hip, ask:
what do you mean, why are you here, what

do you have to offer?, his lips on the verge
of parting.

Singular Duplicity

Asked for the name of a woman with hair
messier than Medusa's, Diego Rivera answered
"Neruda's Mathilda, of course," and painted her
with two heads—undulating auburn hair
long and abundant, like Rita Hayworth's,
two nests of curling serpents
entwined to form the profile
of her poet lover—Pablo of one head.

A master enjoys the licence to deceive
with numerous women and remain
singular, undivided—like my ex, who felt free
to sleep with any female friend or acquaintance
as well as with women he met on ocean voyages,
in bookstores, at conferences and film festivals. While I
became the devious, two-faced cheater
with a single extramarital affair.

"The colour of the glass," Neruda said,
"always changes the taste of the wine."

Visiting Neruda in Valparaiso

Summoned, I enter the dark stairwell,
mount the steep narrow steps,
walls lined with still life fruit
and fowl, the head of a pheasant hanging limp
over the edge of a serving dish.
At the landing I turn toward
the view of harbour and hills—
an extravagance of light
at once ethereal and aquamarine,
almost tactile. He rises from his cloud
and pours Chilean red into green
long-stemmed goblets. "In the desert
of my life," he tells me, as he presses
the liquid to my lips, "you are
my only rose." My knees buckle, I slip
down to kiss his feet but he raises me up
and leads me higher into the stilt house
toward a room suffused with even finer
light, the white of the bedspread
blinding.

But I can't shed my unease
at his penchant for collecting—
not one exotic timepiece but fifty,
not one but thirty paintings
of clipper ships, more than a dozen
full-bosomed figureheads, and countless coloured-glass
goblets, goblets, goblets.
Chances are his habit extends to female flesh,
bone and blood, and I would never be singled out
as one of a kind like the sole carousel pony

centrally displayed for all to see,
the paint on its prancing wooden form
fading.

Catching Myself

At the last moment I caught myself before
tapping that stranger's shoulder, certain it was
you walking down the street in your moccasins
with your cowboy, almost Daliesque moustache,
long scruffy blond hair, work shirt hanging out
over jeans shabby from years of wear, though

years have gone by since your daughter
had the kindness to contact me
and let me know you were dying.

You were the closest I ever came to falling in love
with a dangerous man—drawn in by your tale
of working as a cabdriver, pimping women
to make a little on the side, drawn
to your macho Steve McQueen looks,
the taste of cigarettes on your tongue.

I went weak in the knees seeing you work
with hammer and saw, loved to ride
in the four-wheel-drive
you'd bring in from Torbay where
you lived in a house you'd built yourself
on a cliff overlooking the cove, where
you'd take me surreptitiously
to fuck on the stairs, in the bed,
on the floor, under the table
beneath a cranberry crystal chandelier

But I cringed every time you said "crisises"
for "crises," was sad when you missed references

to Puccini or Nietzsche. You became
the mind/body problem I resolved
in my body's favour on those afternoons
we drove round the bay to where
the sky appears in unrippled ponds,
and pulled off onto the side of the road
and I gave myself over
to the touch of your erudite hands.

The Two Wives of William Holman Hunt

Dickens had a poor opinion
of William Holman Hunt's art
but what dismays me are the lives
of his two wives—Fanny dying
in childbirth, Edith eloping
with her older sister's widower
eight years later, defying
British Common Law and the displeasure
of her mother, Lady Waugh.

The first of Hunt's two portraits of Edith,
with Fanny just out of the picture,
was done on her birthday. She
is gracefully erect, her face serene,
no prescience of future melancholy
but in the head's slight tilt. Her right hand
clutches a fan and a string of amber beads,
her left two roses and a watch on a golden chain.
The whole scene glitters in brilliant oils,
colours of a courting peacock.

The second is in chalk, red and black.
A profile on heavy brown paper,
head bent forward and down
as though pulled by a weight
too heavy for the slender neck thrusting up
out of the soft-collared muslin blouse,
her hair in straggly wisps, her face careworn
from—my guess—traipsing
through the Holy Land, children
in tow, following

her husband's pursuit
of grace, his embrace
of the light of the world.

Ode to David Donnell's *Sometimes a Great Notion*

Cuz these poems run on long-legged
women, beauties who wear,
if anything, loose dresses and are all
mouth. Cuz in scene after scene
he's emerging from the shower before
or after sex. Cuz of omelettes and oysters,
sweet butter and homages to Winona Ryder
(a dust mote he has the audacity to compare
with the incomparable Audrey Hepburn!).
Cuz of allusions to Habermas and Alcibiades
(though I suspect he confuses the Trojan conflict
with the Peloponnesian Wars).
Cuz of these closing lines he gives
to a girlfriend: *You wouldn't believe this stupid
asshole tried to rape me on the subway*—
tossed off as lightly as references
to Schopenhauer, John Ashbery, Coltrane.

It's all so casual and conversational,
so freely associative, anecdotal,
offhand. Even the dark (*days going by
like wild horses*) and the pain (*flopping
like a fish out of water*) are easygoing,
funky. So I can't stay mad.

Michael Snow's *Expo Walking Woman* (1967)

sawed out of brushed and polished steel,
now stands on rods in the AGO's second-floor foyer,
doubled and joined at the back like Siamese twins
driven to stride off in opposite directions
by some impulse operating below
the level of cognition. Another disappears
into empty space framed by the steel sheet
from which she's been excised, her not-thereness
like the ghostly absence
in a photographic negative.

How does she walk
on leg stubs
or carry a notebook,
pen, or purse on arms
amputated at the wrist? Or think
with the crown of her head
sliced off in one clean stroke?
Yet she retains such a jaunty air,
handless arms swinging at her side,
and enjoys iconic replication
cookie cutter fashion
like cutout paper dolls across a page.
I confess

to mellowing over the years since my first
reaction to Walking Woman
with whom I now identify—hobbled
and helpless before the enduring fascination
with dismembering the female body.

Dispute with the Old Poet

The old poet confesses that he wants
"to rub his wrinkles
against smooth skin," a desire shared,
he says, by "virtually *all* aging men,"
meaning no offence
to wizened women. And a younger I,

buried within, wonders how
his firm-fleshed beauties hide
their flinches at his age-spotted,
sagging flesh, knurled joints
and hoary whiskers, imagines
their relief when the game stops
short of shoot and score.

But I myself confess
to the shame and envy
that speak this bitterness:

shame
at my reverberations of distaste
just thinking about undressing
and laying my body down
next to one unlined,
vibrant with youth;

envy
of King David summoning
virginal lovelies to nurse him
in his declining years,
of old Welsh King Math

staving off death by resting
his feet in a virgin's lap,
and of this aging Narcissus
gazing into unclouded eyes
and seeing a younger self
reflected there.

Blow-Up

The front window of this Tim Horton's, backlit
and triptyched, is so clear I feel I'm looking
at an enlarged photograph, a mammoth Jeff Wall, maybe,
of a swath of lawn in a park with trees, leaves
turning, and I'm back in the London
of Antonioni and the many times I returned
to the New Haven cinema to view the film again
bent on resolving whether in one corner of the park
the grass had been pressed down by a dead body
or by two live bodies having sex, but, no, that couldn't be it,
since in the movie's one, for me, unforgettable sex scene,
Sarah Miles lies under a thrusting body on the floor
of some squatted house and looks up, rolling her eyes
and mouthing to a stranger walking by—"I can't wait
for this to be over"—a pantomime like the tennis—*tok, tok*—
played without ball or rackets—*tok, tok*—by white-faced
mimes on a court in that same park, emptiness
and ennui, I think now, some forty years later,
that clarity most likely the point of the film.

Self-Knowledge

You're lying catty-cornered across the bed,
   he complains, and she replies, Yes,

        because I am

catty-cornered, this oblique
     insight striking her
       like the hypotenuse of a triangle.

             Not

that I'm cornered, she thinks,
     or catty (at least not often
       and then only about plagiarists
        and prima donnas).

           No, catty-

cornered as in slantwise, cross-
     hatched, against the grain,
       on a diagonal to the rules,
        at cross purposes

to self and world. But also—
     awareness dawning of the part she plays
       in their petty quarrels—

           crosspatch,

as in captious, prone to wear spleen as well as heart
      on her sleeve, lash out in pique
        and outrage, hiss

and arch her back as she struts
       away
         tail high.

After Life

Volker brought a bottle of Slivovitz and a new girlfriend named Veronica. After dinner, I proposed we all play poker. You became upset when I started introducing one variation after another, and I grew angry with your impatience. I should have stopped with the basics, the hierarchy of winning hands—one pair, two pair, three of a kind, etc. I should never have moved on to seven card stud, the use of wild cards—Jokers, deuces, one-eyed Jacks. Although I don't ordinarily drink hard liquor, the Slivovitz, smooth and viscous with a trace of plum, went down easy. We had polished off the bottle by midnight, and by then a giant moon had hijacked the sky. You and I (Volker and Veronica had by this time slipped away) stepped out of the cottage into a silver-screen world, the night air lit as though with a zillion fireflies. We made our way toward the lake through a low-hanging mist glittering with lunar dust until, transfigured, we became part of that shimmer. Casting my mind back to that night, I'm reminded of *After Life*, the Japanese movie that asks what moment from your life you would choose to live in for all eternity. And I think, well, maybe that one—that moment of transport we wordlessly shared as we walked down to the lake, tipsy with Slivovitz, agog at the gauzy, moon-glistening world, your impatience and my anger folding like a losing poker hand and disappearing beneath the lake's sparkling surface. Yes, it will do.

David Milne Surfacing, 1916

According to this gallery,
that year's palette
was black green white brown,
the latter of a rufous tinge,
usually with snow-like flakes falling,
though within the stippled, piebald scenes
identifiable forms take shape.

In *Woman Painting I*, executed on paper,
through the speckled surface
I make out pencilled tracings
of the folds of a skirt and the unsteady outline
of a woman's profile
as her gaze swings
from easel to vista, vista
to easel,

and barely visible between dabs
of brown white black green
on tan canvas the woman painter
in *Woman in Brown* sitting
camouflaged like the rabbit,
beach ball or wheelbarrow
hidden in a child's cartoon puzzle.

In *Boston Corners*,
white brown green black
applied by brush or palette knife
suffice to suggest road,
three-storey warehouse,
water tank and trees,

and, with heavier reliance
on the green and black
of green black brown white,
I find in *Ferns* and *Bottom of the World*
a myopic view of luxuriant verdure—
gasping, climbing, unfurling,
jostling for a spot of sunlight and soil.

But wait—in another gallery,
here is another Milne
from 1916—*Rocks and Figure*.
In brilliant blue highlights
up from the depths
a woman is reading while reclining
on a rock-strewn shore.

Coming Full Circle

Funny, the way it turned out today—
women and children chatting near the café entrance,
and I, sitting in the room farthest from the door
full of men reading and working on computers—
reminded me of those early '60s medical school parties,
my husband a med student, I embarked
on a master's in history, all the other wives
already mothers or expecting or Home Ec teachers,
and the company always dividing into two camps
like antagonistic ethnic groups except
everyone was WASP, the men
off in one corner talking incomprehensible shop,
the women in another discussing recipes and diapers,
one even boasting she pressed her husband's
undershorts. I was reading the plays
of Georg Büchner—*Dantons Tod, Lenz, Leonce und Lena,*
Woyzeck—and was eager to discuss them but
early 19th-century German *Theaterstücke*
lent themselves to insertion into neither conversation,
and left me falling mute between
megakaryocytes and tuna casserole.

Three Rivers League

On summer evenings they drive
from Moran to Uniontown or Colony,
Pleasanton, Redfield, or Blue Mound,
to sit on teetering wooden bleachers

and watch their daughters play
T ball followed by softball—the shouts
from the sidelines escalating
with the rising level of skill

Caitlin, drop, don't throw
your bat. Roslyn, square up
at the plate. Shauna, get
your glove down.

It's so bucolically rural: the sweet air,
the fireflies beginning to flash
in the increasingly crepuscular light.
This could have been my life

as now, for short visits, I live it
vicariously through two grandnieces,
as their mother and father devote
(once I would have thought sacrifice)

evenings to chauffeuring their girls
and volunteering to coach or sit
in the dugout and keep score or serve
as umpire at first base. I myself

played ball growing up, though I was never
taught as these girls have been
how not to throw like a girl, and as an adult
I never forfeited my own ambitions

for the sake of helping daughters
acquire such skills. I'm not at all sure
I would do it differently
if I had it to do over, but at 72,

in the cooling air, I cheer
my grandnieces from the sidelines—
Nice catch, Emily. Good slide,
Clara. Go on anything!

Dear Richard

I believe in saying it all
and taking it all back

and saying it again for good measure,
while the air fills up with *I'm-Sorries*

like wheeling birds
and the trees look seasick in the wind.

Tony Hoagland

A Hard Nut

"That's it in a nutshell": Dad
summing up. I pictured the crux of an argument
enclosed in a walnut's cranium-like husk
stripped of pith with that sharp instrument one
might mistake for a crochet hook. Our nutcracker
came with a set of four such picks, one for each of us,
and we used them that evening, sitting around the table,
cracking open and prying out the meat from the walnuts
Dad had brought home as a treat. But soon Richard,
sated, bored, started tickling—poking me between the ribs,
scrabbling with his fingers under my arms until, laughing
uncontrollably, I began to weep, and Mom and Dad, nerves
shot, ordered us to stop. Tears after mirth: non sequitur.
My childhood in a nutshell.

My Mother's Daughter

Hardly a week went by without Mom brandishing
pages of faded sheet music from a faux-Hawaiian band—
a picture of her, demure, on the cover, wearing a lei,
cradling a ukulele, hair in a Louise Brooks bob. She'd declare:
"I could have gone on the stage and become
a famous singer, if it hadn't been
for the two of you."

I was well into my twenties before I finally did the math:
married in April '27, son born October '34,
daughter February '38.
Seven childless, stay-at-home years
that, by all signs, she devoted
to becoming Betty Crocker. Her kitchen

a mini-factory in summer: mason jars
rattling in canners on the stove,
clarified blackberry and boysenberry juice
dripping through cheesecloth bags. Smell
of hot paraffin sealing the jars to be stacked
on basement shelves, preserving
the harvest off her brothers'
Yakima farm—pears, peaches, apricots, plums
fluorescent as the bones
in our feet viewed through the Bon Marché's
X-ray shoe-fitting machine.

I was spared the steamy work of canning,
shooed out of doors into the summer sun,
never required to learn those now-esoteric skills,
only called in for a slice of bread spread with the foam

skimmed off the top of still-warm jellies and jams
and devoured just as unthinkingly as I swallowed
the potent mix of guilt and vicarious ambition.

Unwise

Sophistication started out
a spin-off from sophistry
itself derived from *Sophia*—the word
for wisdom in Greek but also
a given name often given
to a woman as in *Sophie's Choice*
a novel William Styron wrote
in the aftershock of Treblinka
Buchenwald, Chelmo and the rest.

Mention sophisticates and I see
Myrna Loy, William Powell, Hollywood's
Nick and Nora Charles casually
sipping their daily dozen martinis
while stick-handling repartee
like ricocheting bullets, the agility
of their banter only matched

by the casuistry I encountered
a short month after the wedding
when I awoke to my mistake and
seeking escape, visited my brother
to confide my anguish at realizing
too late the man I married and I
were not soulmates. Agreeing
my Jesuit scholastic sibling
in the Spokane Philosophate
offered help until he

discovering I had, when a teenager,
been baptized, did a volte-
face—the possibility of annulment
suddenly annulled by the insistence
on submission to a sacrament even
a Congregationalist baptism certified
so neither certificate could be torn up
like a forgiven traffic ticket or dissolved
like Alka-Seltzer in a glass of water
however Jesuitical and sophisticated
the sophistry.

Dear Richard

It was wartime and back behind the house
in the Victory garden on Phinney Bay
our parents kept chickens
that mother deftly beheaded.

"This chicken," you quipped one Sunday
as the platter was passed,
"has too many legs—I count four."
My plate crashed to the floor
as I ran from the table.

Years later you insisted
Blackie was *your* pet,
as if that made a difference.

A decade or so later still,
in an eleven-page single-spaced letter
of venomous accusation and attack,
you screamed at me: *You think
everything revolves around you.*

I should have listened then
to my friend Thelma.
Dear Richard,
she advised me to write,
you can keep the rabbit.

Alike and Not Alike

Just as I was throwing on my coat,
you threw out:
"We're a lot alike, don't you think?"

Caught off guard, I answered, *yes*, hyper-aware
for the moment, of those interests I acquired
looking up to you in my teens and early twenties,
bending myself in a scholarly direction
to replicate your intellectual bent.

What other young woman among my friends
studied the Church Fathers and the Scholastics
to impress an older brother,
or flirted with mysticism after reading Evelyn Underhill,
imagining herself locked away in a closet,
God-intoxicated, merged with the All?

While you became a priest, religion soured
on me, women's place in it so markedly
subordinate, except for a Teresa of Avila
or the inimitable, alone-of-all-her-sex
Virgin Mother.

Temperamentally similar, you and I? Yes, but
you were more intense, higher strung.
With one leg crossed over the other, you could never
sit still, top leg jumping like a puppy on speed.

And did I never notice your aloneness in high school
when I had a gang of friends and you had one,
Dennis, whom you lent me to teach

ten of my closest how to Charleston
for our annual vaudeville show.

Twine and Rouge

Do you remember standing at the hub
and leading me, tied to a length
of whipping twine and led
around in a circle like a horse
urged from walk to trot. I teetered
breaking in my first high heels,
but you, my trainer, assured me I'd learn
balance in time. And do you remember
the pancake makeup, lipstick and rouge
you painted on my face giving it
a more mature look than its thirteen years.
But that was all before, donning black
and clerical collar, you forswore
frivolity, wanting us both

hitched to a tauter lead.

First Cause

And then there's the time Mom and Dad,
visiting in Newfoundland,
were recalling their first year of parenthood—
how you cried without let-up

and how one evening they went to bed
exhausted, so thoroughly worn out
they slept the whole night through
and woke the next morning to discover
your voice completely gone.

What a revelation, I thought then
and still think now, wondering
whether that was the source
of your sense of abandonment,
the germ of your need
for a heavenly father.

After Jack Chambers' *McGilvary County*

Parcel of paradise, slice
of the big rock candy mountain,
corner of Cockaigne where lemon-
yellow suns and Persian blue spheres
revolve in the sky like haloed
planets from a friendly distant galaxy
and the heads of the county's elders
bob in the heavens like bodiless
Fra Angelico or Perugino putti.
Green cone-like trees line the ridges
of hills coated in powdered sugar,
the valley brims with phantasmagoric
abundance, its grass buried under a rioting
insinuation of roses and daisies.
Teapots, grape-bearing epergnes, bowls of berries,
delicate pastries pyramided atop plates,
a pestle and mortar, seven shining eggs,
a coffee grinder, cup and saucer, platters
of peaches, apricots and pears—all drenched
in glittering sunshine—a vision of childhood
in full-colour Kodachrome dreamt
by someone blessed with memories
of growing up fussed over—or else the fantasy
of one unloved from birth and haunted
by an insatiable longing to have been lavished
as a child with birthday parties
and mouth-watering picnics on the grass
hovered over by doting aunts and uncles.
The whole bountiful mise-en-scène
projected in thick squalls of paint
onto a Roman shade pulled down to within an inch

of a window sill, tassels hanging
motionless in the static air.

Among the Dahlias

I have always sided with Antigone,
not her sister Ismene,
who believed the gods granted men
power over women. But our father,
who rejected you as Creon
renounced Polyneices,
was no tyrant to me.
Only occasionally did I resent
his rulings—not letting me go
on hunting expeditions, or play
poker with his pals.
He did teach me how to fish
and I was thrilled when he took me,
and not asthmatic you,
to Seattle Rainiers' games
where we'd sit in the bleachers eating
peanuts and crackerjacks. And he accepted
my checkered marital career while,

in the theatre of my life, you enacted the roles
of both beloved Polyneices and
authoritarian Creon, censorious
of my divorces, my living "in sin."
At thirteen, I was horrified
at your church's policy of sacrificing
the mother for the sake of the infant
if only one could be saved. When I said so,
you chastised me, citing Aquinas,
as we stood arguing among mother's dahlias.
Was it fear born of that exchange
that kept me from having children? If so,

unlike Antigone, my defiance didn't cost me
my life, just the possibility of one day
hearing children of my own argue
life and death among the dahlias.

Our Rec Room

Knotty-pine panelled, reached
off the kitchen. A battered upright
piano to the left of steep, uncarpeted stairs;
on their right, tucked away, a row of stools
cozied up to the bar. Two couches, salvaged
from the Sally Ann, faced off
before the fireplace on the far wall.

We kept a portable phonograph down there
and played our 78s and 33s
at top volume, taking no notice of scratches
in the shellac, gouges in the grooves—*Guys
and Dolls, South Pacific, New Faces of 1951,
Brigadoon.* It was where we all gathered,

Mom and Dad, you and I, to watch on our first TV
the Army/McCarthy hearings
(mother shocked not by the Senator's
politics but by his catholic use
of profanity) and the New York City Ballet
dancing *Rodeo*, Bernstein conducting
astride a bucking horse. Without Alistair Cooke's

Sunday telecasts devoted to the arts,
could you and I ever have dreamt of escape
to where not everyone grows china plate dahlias
and—except that one time Dad came home late,
staggering from the car, tie loosened, shoes unlaced—
        all families sit down to dinner at six sharp.

In the Moment

Loosed from routine
of morning juice and coffee, afternoon
tea and toast, evening news,
I stroll the shore, pocketing stones
and silvered pieces of driftwood, touching
the shine of rain on lacecap hydrangeas,
watching black-tined crows rake the air.

Pang of return after a long
absence to a place ghosted,
echoic. But when sun shreds
the cloud tarpaulin,
glorious Mount Rainier rises
as though by parthenogenesis.

That this sight will continue
into tomorrows I'll never see
should console, not occasion
the bronchial, scapular ache
of envy. I should live in the moment,
like Aunt Louise at 97. "Look!

at the table," she exclaims,
how its glass top catches the sky!"

Dilemma

I was resolved to sell
the cedar-sentinelled wedge
of riverbank land,
fern shocks fringing
our parents' mock log cabin,
but I've returned to Toronto
with nothing decided.

Ownership, taxes, repairs—
they fell to me, not you,
priest pledged to poverty and now retired
to a small parish a few hours by car and ferry
from the summer idyll of our childhood
you cherish as much as I.
Has it become for you a proxy
for home and intimacy renounced
as Jesuit, a servant's pull
connecting you to me, your sister,
thousands of miles away?
I wanted out.

But on the first morning back,
as I descended the stone steps
to the river's edge, the sun,
glancing off the water,
pierced me with all those summers
we vacationed on the banks
of the tumbling stream Dad fished
with rod and reel, and the cousins and I,
in an exercise in futility, set out
barefoot every June to dam—

this guttering-over-rock that remains,
though merely a brook,
the river of my dreams.

Facings

"When others asked the truth of me, I was convinced it was not the truth they wanted, but an illusion they could bear to live with."
—Anaïs Nin, writer (1903–1977)

"The abstraction is often the most definite form for the intangible thing in myself that I can only clarify in paint."
—Georgia O'Keefe, painter (1887–1986)

Some might say Nin's statement has the ring
of truth as though truth were the sound
a bell intones

Others might say it contains a grain
or a kernel of truth as if *veritas*
needs husking or threshing

But what if truth is like O'Keefe's abstraction: a definite form
for an intangible something inside yourself
that you can only clarify in paint or, in a poet's case, words

Or perhaps one person's truth is another's illusion
and our act of love is to perform for our friends
the illusions they require of us

Arguably truth is something that can only be tested
or distilled or clarified in moments
of unsurpassed extremity

as, for instance, *im Angesicht des Todes*,
or in the face of birth or maybe beauty,
unmistakable beauty

Presumably Nin believed she knew a truth or truths
about herself she kept buried to shield
either herself from her friends or them from her

I suspect my own truth or truths
are like the razor clams on Hood Canal beaches
instinctually aware, as the clam digger approaches

of the need for a swift descent
burrowing through layers of sand
to deeper, more unreachable depths

Better Never

Those afflicted with chronic, as distinct from acute,
leukemia, can live for a decade or more.
So say the medical books.
And you were always a complainer.
Once in a letter you groused
about too many of your parishioners
whinging like wounded animals.
Then came the diagnosis—
pancreatic cancer.
And we barely had time.

Fear played a part in my failure to come
until almost too late. Not a wimp's fear,
but that of a puppy whipped once too often.
So did my cussedness, my *I'll be damned*
before I give him another chance
to make me cringe with guilt.
Priest, pedant, resentful yet lonely brother—
such a gift you had for making me feel
wretched, so angry more than once
I could have killed you.

Those last days together, after the first shock
of seeing your haggard body, were a gift.
We were stiff and wary with one another
until we opened a bottle of bubbly at 11:00 a.m.
and drank from borrowed crystal flutes,
frolicking our way through dozens of loved topics
like quiz show whiz kids on a spree. Relieved,
we could have donned party hats
and turned somersaults on the lawn had I
not been seventy and you not deathly ill.

Visiting a Dying Brother

the body of a bird
lying on the sidewalk
another in the hospital parking lot
feathers and bones
crushed on asphalt
wings spread flat
silvering into heraldry

your body
the shock of your body
slivering toward skeletal, skin
translucent as our mother's
Belleek, muscle and fat
melted away like the rancour
of all those now
meaningless quarrels, mutual
recriminations

a friend says
when I show her your photo
what a sweet face

Passus Est

For as a man lives, he dies,
Ashbery wrote, quoting
someone. Is that true?
There was the occasional flash
of prickly impatience over a drug
misplaced, a call missed, or a book
misshelved, but, dying,
you were, on the whole,

the epitome of kindness, even sweetness
to your sister, parishioners, caregivers.
After your knee-jerk decision to fight
came calm acceptance, even embrace
of the fast-approaching end, curtain
more final than for any of those plays
you once performed in—*Love's Labour's Lost,*
Oedipus Rex, Oedipus at Colonus—
all that forgotten at the last, folded
into a focus on gratitude and concern
for those who surrounded you
as you endured the relentless pain
of those terminal days,

a suffering to which your Church assigns
great spiritual value, as I read today
in the *Sunday Star*, about the Toronto Archdiocese
campaigning to canonize
Sister Carmelina Tarantino
whose decades-long suffering drew
petitioners to her bedside in droves
for counsel, blessing, intercession.

When after our long estrangement,
I saw you again I blurted
that I thought you were dying
very well. Meaning your fortitude
was saintly, not that you had become
someone to pray to. Oh, no, dear Richard.
Far too great a leap.

Flowers for the Dead and Dying

What is the exact name
of those white and pink cornets
flaring at the end of curved branches
I see growing along Roncesvalles—
trumpeting angels, angels' trumpets?

I think of Roland winding his horn
as he lay dying on the legendary pass,
and I hear trumpets sounding on Judgment Day,
and still I resent these beauties
blooming in the face of your dying.

Why didn't I ask what was in your mind
all those years ago when,
after scattering our mother's ashes
around the summer cabin,
you planted a myriad frilled marigolds,

orange and yellow and mute.

A Little Knowledge

In those final days, we never talked about our mom and dad,
not even about our years of growing up under the same roof,
our together years, so to speak, and certainly not about our quarrels,
frequent and fierce as two blue jays at a feeder. No mention

of your asthma and my irrepressibly good health,
my boundless energy and youthful love of life
diluted only by a dim awareness that something
was amiss—Dad taking me, not you, to the games,
his fury at finding *A Girl of the Limberlost* among your books,
you, with the genius IQ, I, the mere over-achiever.

Not one word about Mom's heartbreak at your decision
to go over to the papists and become a priest and her agonizing
obsession with who had seduced you, led you astray, or about her agony
for years, her face blanching whenever someone mentioned
your name, despite my repeated efforts to assure her
that the Jesuits were the guardians of doctrinal truth,
the most respected, best educated, most intellectual and highly regarded

order in the Roman Church, arguing how much better it was
to be a servant of God, whether Catholic or Protestant, than, say,
bank robber or rapist, or even actor, the other profession
you must have considered, a scarier choice it no doubt seemed
than joining an all-male community of the like-minded.
How little we knew back then.

Forgive and Forget

1

Wherever you went, you told me,
during one of our final visits,
you carried with you
a copy of my first book of poems.
You said you found forgiveness in it
for my womanizing ex-husband,
and asked whether that was true. No, I replied,

I'm not the forgiving sort, I was only conceding
my part. You were really asking whether
I forgave you, I knew, and I should have said
yes.

I have forgiven you, but I cannot forget
you once wrote *if you were Jewish,*
you'd be called a J.A.P., Jewish American
Princess—you spelled it out, then
meticulously defined: a female
not only spoiled but totally self-
centred, utterly
incapable of thinking
of others.

What for years I couldn't forgive
is the kernel of truth in that.
Yet it was inevitable I would eventually forgive
the you who carried around a book of my poems
like a rare edition of Augustine's *City of God*.

But for failing to say, out loud,
before you died,
you have my forgiveness,
as I was able to say
you have my love,
how do I forgive myself?

2

To think I was the only one to forgive,
with nothing to be forgiven for!

I had forgotten my fury
at Dad's funeral,

unleashed by your decision
to put his corpse on view
(I wanted to remember him alive
holding a brace of ducks or
a stringer of rainbow trout),

fanned by your remark
at the funeral dinner,
about his weakness
for full-breasted women
when everyone present knew our mother
had breasts like an underfed pigeon,

a fury near full force when you asked
for his letter opener as keepsake
of the untold times you helped open his mail
in the months before he died, which,
my rage by then at blizzard pitch,
I refused.

Now I live
with its cutlass-blade smile
of reproach.

Louise Berliawsky Nevelson's *Night Zag IV* (1945)

A sharp turn through the film noir chambers
of the mind, dark cubicles of the heart, memory's
rubbish bins, a wooden cabinet of curios
painted matte-black like the shadowed
space between breaths, unlit cafés,
the bevelled edges of loss, sculpted legs
of repressed desire. Four joined
columns of packing crates stacked
five high—some boarded up, some glass-
fronted like our grandmother's ebony hutch—
rise from a weighted base of cubes into
a pulsing syncopation of discord
jammed with life's helter-skelter—cogs
and cylinders from torpedoed plans,
obsolescent fantasies, spindles and spools,
oversize pepper grinders, rolling pins,
flywheels, chests for chloroformed moths,
tobacco tins, oil cans, batons and truncheons,
soiled typewriter ribbons—all patched
together into a farrago of those maybes
and nos and if onlys, a monument
to abjection, lapse and angst climbing
my bedroom wall every night, case
upon crammed case, to stand in mocking
judgment on inattention and impatience,
on my fault-finding tongue and my failure
to forgive, a barbiturate-tight bulwark
against sinking into untroubled sleep.

More Than Regret

The last of the aspen leaves
detach themselves and fall, leaves I celebrated
when they were turning the sun's yellow
into green. Now in autumn they've returned
to yellow, not the sun's, but a shade more abashed,
tinged with mustard and regret. And
also shame—at my reluctance
to acknowledge your flourishing, so tightly
did I cling to my sense of inferiority,
my envy of your intellectual prowess,
my fear of your priestly rectitude.
Even in those final days, swathed
in self-protective gear and steeped
in self-righteousness, I failed
to fathom the devotion you had won
from parishioners who stood in line
to give you care both night and day,
cherished your persnicketiness
as one of many endearing traits.
In her letter of condolence
the church secretary wrote
that you wept after my every visit.

Likenesses

A dense wood encircles the church where you ministered for a decade,
the trees pressing in on the glass-walled sanctuary, faithful parishioners
leaning forward to catch your every word. The squirrel's nest
in the highest branches of that maple, like your cancer,
invisible until the leaves fell.

Today, with autumn's blaze extinguished, the maples stand bare
amidst their conifer cousins, abandoned
to the season's melancholy,
the ground sodden with brown leaves
slowly breaking down.

the day before your funeral

Snoqualmie River
swollen after weeks of heavy rain

roads flooded
fields gullywashed
a salmon seen crossing the interstate

Snoqualmie Falls
once a long swooshing flow
like Rapunzel's hair let down
now a thundering cataract

barely visible through downpour
and bursts of dense mist
erupting from the crash
of water on water

the river a muddy masala
churning and cresting
along a seam of roiling froth

huge logs plunging over the edge
swiftly swallowed into roar
the day before your funeral

The Evening of Your Funeral

Flaunting its radiance
the pock-cheeked moon, eyes
unblinking, rises brazen above the trees
into a sky of preternatural clarity.

The funeral director dragoons me
into helping him *tuck in the body*,
his words. My own body on loan
to a self unwillingly cast in this role,
my hand slipping onto the cardboard
stiffness of what once was your chest.

White chasuble over cinctured alb,
a final flourish of red stole,
the procession of priestly regalia,
archdiocesan and Jesuit,
begins its solemn march

into a sanctuary ablaze with light
and wafting incense, Dwight
and I in the pallbearers' wake
stumbling through the un-
familiar liturgy.

After the mass, the Reverend Fathers
lift your coffin into the hearse.
One thrusts into my hands
a vial of holy water, shows me
how it should be swung
to disperse drops over the casket,

and I look on as my body,
shivering in the yet clear
but now cooler, darker air,
obediently performs its assigned task.

After Betty Goodwin's *The Memory of the Body* (1993)

As Whitman sang the body electric
Goodwin sings the body forested:
dense stand of dark-trunked saplings
illumined by a blood-streaked sky,
ominous forest where
abandoned children wander
vulnerable to the spell of wolves,
stepmothers and jealous queens—
omnivorous forest, perilous to enter.

I mean the body unseen,
the body beneath the skin
where invisible infrastructure
thrums as it surges and sluices
through murky runnels and canals, networks
of branching pipes puffing,
slaving away—*schuften*,
schuften, schuften, schuften—
with little or no compensation
until strength gives out, and
the blood-orange sea explodes,
subsides, drains away

or is pumped clean by funereal technicians
like those who flushed and sewed
until your body became the one
displayed in the satin-lined casket,
a papier-mâché effigy wearing
your wire spectacles—

not a body I recognized,
not the body you inhabited as a boy
small for your age, red-nosed, recurrently
bedridden, a body we believed
had no athletic bent, the body you left

behind as you grew into manhood
discovering the body turning
handsprings in *Love's Labour's Lost*
as we gasped in disbelief, having
been firm in our conviction that your body

was incapable of anything more
physical than some side stroke swimming, yet
here you were, suddenly fit and muscled,
dancer-like in strength and grace,

in an adult body that filled out over the years,
acquired padding traceable to your priestly
passion for food and drink, especially fine
non-sacerdotal wine—a fullness
cancers and their ruthless treatments
then eroded, sucking

vitality from your cheeks and bones—the frame
over which morticians pulled
your tissue-thin skin to fashion
a caricature of your vacated body,
the body I wish to erase from my memory,
the body I refuse as the memory of you.

As if I Were Antigone

I collect fallen leaves off the mountain path,
dried cones from fir and larch,
and grey speckled pebbles
as if gathering loose earth
for a brother's grave,
but I have no need to scratch
from the hard ground enough dry dust
to pile a burial mound,
nor to defy a tyrant's sentence of death
for disobeying his decree—all subjects
to leave Polyneices unburied,
his corpse a rich sweet sight for hungry birds—
for you shall be neither untombed nor unwept.

a grieving walk (Chile)

angry clang of metal fence
curmudgeon crunch of gravel underfoot
a dog's yawning growl
how dare the sky revel in such halleluiah blue
gripped by sadness, I lower my eyes
and concentrate instead on my feet stepping
onto the dirt path caked hard as a casket lid
the ditch full of thin weeds like puny strands of hair
braided too tight   trees drop round, sharply knobbed
seed pods like balls on the end of a torturer's chain

I still have last night's headache/heartache

heartache/headache—the power lines pulse

like an agitated dressmaker's sewing machine
the grape vines are tied to their poles'
with blue plastic bands like hospital bracelets
the edges of the grape leaves serrated like knives
I taste the shadow of a hawk on my tongue
run my hand down the blistered bark of the juniper
pick a misshapen pear the hue of a day-old bruise
sit down by a discarded tire lying flat at the base of a tree
pick up a length of twine looped like a hanging rope
hear overhead the endlessly carping queltehue
prick my hand on an espino thorn

skinflint pain, no expiation
for your death

A Particulate Blackness

I switch on the bedside light and pick up my book,
knowing these tactics will merely delay the return
of the black particles that fly at me, swerving
at the last moment only to turn back and rush at me again.

What is it I fear? Not death itself, but the manner
in which you died—wasting away to such unbearable thinness
two months before the end you hadn't enough flesh
to pinch together and sink a needle into.

At your funeral, a fellow Jesuit reminded me
of the heart trouble you'd suffered in graduate school
struggling to complete that stillborn doctoral thesis.
I needed no reminder of the time you collapsed while leading
a retreat for nuns in a town east of Los Angeles,
my friend Martha driving me through sun-seared hills

to where you lay in hospital, in the care of Sisters,
one of whom scratched at my door to tell me, absent
from Mass, that my agnosticism lay at the heart of your attack.
You swore you hadn't put her up to it, but at the time,
furious, I was sure you shared her belief. I still smart

from the charge—irrationally wondering if I *could*
be responsible for all the troubled sadness in your life.
I used to pray you would not become Pope, fearful that if you did
I would be unable to withstand the pressure to convert.

It's hard now to believe we enjoyed a halcyon interlude
when you gleefully spoke of the future Pope as she
who would make abortion a sacrament, both of us laughing,

half believing it could happen. Then later you accused me
of having led you into liberal heresies, astray.

During the Novitiate years, on your occasional visits home,
when you drove me around in our parents' car,
I, incarnation of the female sex,
Jezebel the temptress, Eve the midwife of evil,
had to sit in the back seat.

Four Months and Fourteen Days

Since I don't believe in life after death,
a spirit world to which you have gone—
I dismiss such superstitions—why then
do I carry on these posthumous conversations
with you who occupy my thoughts
even more than when you were alive.
Why do I worry you might, from wherever
you now reside, be looking down—down!—
and seeing me at whatever I'm doing. The other evening
as I soaked in the bath, this fear entered me
bringing instant shame, instant recall
of the psychotherapist fascinated
with the "gender confusion"
of our upbringing—
incestuous, she said,
your zealous interest in my soul, claiming
to have spotted the very word
in one of your letters from a batch I let her see,
though I've searched and searched
and never found it.

Once I flew to Chicago to visit friends and you drove
from Milwaukee to pick me up—you had been begging me
to let you take me out to lunch—and afterward not only
dropped me at my friends' house
but walked me to their door.
Glancing back through the glass,
I saw a look on your face so
nakedly bereft I felt I had somehow cruelly
let you down. I am not your wife, I said to myself,
and kept repeating like a spell:

not your wife, not your sweetheart,
not your best friend.
I am only your sister.

The Symbolical Real

(After Elaine Whittaker's *Tether*, 2009)

For a time she planned
to use in her art installation
the actual red plaid
robe her father wore
in the days before he died,
but an insuperable
sense of trespass
led her to hang instead
a black and white
photograph of it.

I understand.
I'm ill at ease handling
the few books I received
from your small library—
American Heritage Dictionary,
latest edition; the *OED*; and the *Oxford
Dictionary of the Christian Church*,

which you studiously consulted
during one of my last visits,
helping me amend a poetic reference
to the Great Schism of 1054.

Now holding that book in my hands
I feel your fingers searching through its pages
and am overcome by the imbalance of things—
my acquisitiveness, your poverty,
my marriages, your celibacy,

my defiance of rules, your obedience,
my handful of poems, your sermons and prayers,

your dying, my continuing to live.

Seesaw

That final email you sent, giddy
with a false sense of reprieve, haunts me—
a near miraculous increase in platelets,
the bone marrow extraction cancelled.
At the end you burbled, *I would*
have been arrested for drunk driving.
Good thing someone else was there
to drive you home.

In that moment you briefly reversed
the pattern of our growing up years—
I, the perpetual motion machine,
you, the sickly asthmatic excused
from playing sports in dusty gyms,
from mowing the lawn and joining
the Boy Scouts.

Even muddling through my middle years—
taking Prozac on doctor's orders,
contemplating suicide—I had no
legitimate claim to despondency.
Disappointment, discontent,
yes, but not serious depression,
your exclusive franchise.

Now, I feel more than ever obliged
to live life feverishly, in some eyes
the Energizer Bunny in caricature,
courting the return of chronic fatigue,
packing every hour with at least a show
of joie de vivre, under pressure to find delight

even on a damp, miserable day like today—and I do,
often in the smallest things,
like the concentric circles raindrops
trace in puddled asphalt,
the glistening beads of water
forming on umbrellas tops,
the lone sparrow sporadically foraging
up and down this café's
deserted patio.

Heat Wave

a misnomer for this sodden hogwash, wa-
sabi hot, smothering the city—June, July,
August—no end in sight. Waves, after all,

abate—like those heard on cool
Phinney Bay summer nights, stars
falling through a Van Gogh sky to the slap,
slurp, slap of passing craft. Now,

in this land-locked urban space, the forecast "un-
abated" chafes. A straw that breaks—

that's what I crave. Also wane and ebb,
finitude: the day lily's swift
wilt, stars dying before we see their light.

That window's double-glazed pane,
this rock.
A slow shattering.

One Year Later

A year ago, as you awaited death, I stumbled
through Toronto's fall
film festival in a state of shock
like sudden loss of oxygen,
and guiltily sat in the dark indulging
my passion for images moving
across the screen—tumbling clouds, mist
rising off a river, a woman's face
distorted in ecstasy or sorrow—and this fall
attending the same festival,
and reading as I stand in line waiting
for the next film to begin, I'm halted
mid-page

by the word "polytheism" and the memory
of the time you were immured
in your novitiate and I,
with my Protestant roots,
studying medieval Europe at university—
its history so largely that of the Roman Church—
was confused by the multitude of saints
and the high rank accorded the Virgin Mary,
Queen of Heaven, Mother of God.
It seemed almost as polytheistic
as the Hindu pantheon
or that of ancient Greece,
so I wrote you, asking for clarification
and in return received a harsh rebuke
for my ignorance of devotion's hierarchy—
veneration, adoration, worship—
each grade of sacredness assigned a different rung,

the highest reserved exclusively
for three-personed God.

I have grown to appreciate
belief systems capacious enough for a host
of holy beings, regardless
of their sacred status, high or low,
the lonely God of Luther, Calvin and Zwingli so
austere, so like a meal of bread and water
as compared with *Babette's Feast*, a movie you
read as allegory of the richness of Catholicism
in contrast with pietistic parsimony, thus subverting
my enjoyment of that film for years.

Falling

"For at twilight each voyage is, in fact, our requiem,
the same as dreams are cubbyholes
in which are stuffed, over and over, our seasons

of poems and prayers, as a key may turn in a lock,
a step on a stair, till one fine morning we'll meet ourselves
deep in the roaring dark, and face our graves at last."

Robert Mazzacco

Supplication

Forgive us our infelicities and addictions
coffee shops and haute couture, co-dependencies
and all that is petroleum-derived and -driven

Forgive us our cork-skewed values, our callous
calculations, our hierarchies and exclusions
our cockamamie homilies and blunt forgetfulness

Forgive us our whinnying self-mortifications
our narcissistic lack of self-awareness
our poker-faced accusatory self-regard

Detour us neither into greener pastures
nor deserts of despond
but skyward into delirious promiscuities

and impromptu acts of exculpation

Dancing at the Edge

In the Middle Ages prancing Death
led a chain of dancers drawn
from every rank, peasant to Kaiser, beggar to Pope.

Tonight spruce are silhouetted across the horizon
like the *danse macabre* in *The Seventh Seal.*
The moonlit night before Palm Sunday

in March '42, Lancasters over Lübeck
bombed the Marienkirche's *Totentanz* fresco
to ash. In the new

millennium Death,
still playing his bone fiddle, extends
his invitation to polar bears and Venice, emperor

penguins, white and black spruce,
lodgepole pine, the dancers picked democratically
just as in the past, for this their last

shuffle—skeleton-led, ramshackle, rakish.

Portent and After-Image

(After Paterson Ewen's *Halley's Comet as Seen by Giotto*, 1979)

Unaware Europe sent *Giotto* into space
with cameras to beam back images,
I simply assumed the Giotto
of Ewen's *Halley's Comet*
was the celebrated early Renaissance master,
an easy assumption since his blue
echoes the lapis lazuli luminescence
of Giotto's star-spangled skies frescoed
onto the ceiling vault and walls
of Padua's Scrovegni Chapel.

I missed Halley's Comet in 1986
and won't be alive for its next showing
in 2062. But its sighting in 1910
was a highlight of my mother's
West Virginian childhood.
So it seems not impossible Giotto
could have witnessed a visitation.

Clearly Ewen shared Giotto's passion
for stars and other celestial phenomena.
Lightning streaks across his landscapes
the way angels sweep across Giotto's heavens,
and Halley's Comet as observed by his *Giotto*
blazes across a router-gouged blue-stained sky
like divine revelation or prolonged electric shock,
its flaming tail the campanile of Firenze's Duomo,

an umbilical cord looping back to the Tricento's first half,
that proliferation of dukedoms, principalities and city states,
painters, bankers, silversmiths, clog-
shod weavers, paper makers, and condottieri,
a world barely beginning to ascend out of a long darkness
only to be *smote* as if by a meteoric
maelstrom, its population more than decimated
by deadly plague recurrent for lifetimes to come.

Josef Sudek's *Egg, Glass Still Life* (ca. 1950)

A photograph (gelatin silver print)
of the absolute perfection of an egg's
ovalness, the perfect roundness of
a shallow white saucer, the sheer simplicity
of dark coffee in a clear glass—all resting
pristine on a dark-grained wooden board
or tray, or maybe a short counter
just broad enough to hold the saucer's
umbra and also the shadowed underside
of the egg where it rests on the saucer's edge,
tilting as eggs do when we lay them down
on a hard curved surface—the egg
not white or brown but beigy-tan and
slightly speckled—hard-boiled, we assume,
a coffee-and-egg breakfast for a man
in a very manly arrangement—the elemental
starkness, the lack of fuss—
and it was photographed by a man,
a Czech, Josef Sudek, sometime
around 1950, when he was living
in a post-war Czechoslovakia
already under Soviet control—
a time of austerity, of thwarted recovery, indeed
a time of deprivation for many, but not,
for just this moment, for the recipient of the egg
and coffee on a clean white saucer, still one
of the lucky few, for fortunes change so swiftly,
a reason to savour whatever good fortune
comes your way and hope you won't have
to sell your soul—see Czeslaw Milosz's
The Captive Mind—and I'm thinking

of the things we do to stay among the favoured
and I don't mean on the side of the angels
but how we look the other way, eat
our perfectly prepared egg, drink our imported coffee,
having carefully captured both
to secure with black photo corners
in the album of our life.

Thesis, Antithesis

(After Jack Gilbert's "A Brief for the Defense")

Follow the pilgrim's path
from one prayer station to the next,
each a kind of roadside shrine crossed
with peak-roofed birdhouse. Sing
a Franciscan canticle to the blond-

and ash-brown-whiskered hills
glinting in sun-glossed hoarfrost,
their rounded curves and hollows
like the shoulders and haunches of bison
that once grazed and galloped here.
But other images intrude—

a father cradling his boy killed
by a bomb dropped on Falluja. A mother
slowly dying of AIDS in Nairobi. Orphans
picking through garbage on the outskirts
of Rio. And yet a favourite poet seems

to argue that the well-off are obliged to enjoy
their good fortune, a pole star
to the sufferings of others,
the unfortunate who otherwise . . .

would be none the wiser?
Seductive reasoning. A pretty
dialectic—Panglossian optimism
or Niebuhr's prayer for the courage
to change what we can

and accept what we cannot.
Are these our only choices?
Withdrawal to cultivate one's own garden
or serenity dependent on faith?
How we scramble

and scrounge to reconcile ourselves
to lives fortressed against earth's hells
while the indifferent hills sprawl
in the lustre of the morning sun
and don't twitch a muscle.

Josef Sudek's *Window of My Studio with Blossom* (1950)

"To articulate or to interpret?"—
as though one came without the other.

Unremarkable—small, sepia in tone
and awash in misty insubstantiality.
No wonder it hangs on the far wall
at the far end of the AGO's first floor.
Even when I look more closely
I first miss the numinous focus
of the print—a blossoming branch
stuck in a water glass on a window sill
overshadowed by the hazy scene outside
aswim in shapes so indistinct, so ghostly,
that only with effort do I make out the hint
of a chimney rising from a roof
and a dark Kandinsky-like bolt
scoring the slant of the blossoming twig.

Spring's promise of renewal or
gloom gathering over Prague?

By Any Other Name

Zerbrechlich and early to wither
but prolific and wildly self-seeding
their fragile stalks fringe
the shade garden with a flutter
of lacy celadon green leaves
from whose midst thin shoots
dangle rows of heart-shaped charms
red tapering to a prism of white

Whether you perceive these
delicate baubles to be tears
from weeping hearts—*tränende Herzen*
the German etiquette—or pearls of blood
from a bleeding heart—the English—
could be a matter of nomenclature
stemming from cultural disparities
between idealism and materialism
the metaphysician and the shopkeeper

But I prefer a centuries-old tale
of a recently widowed woman
out gathering herbs in a shady wood
espying these blooms and thinking
blood dripping from a wounded heart
while across the channel in a village
edged by a similar forest, another woman
grieving the recent loss of a child
and seeing the same blooms thought

hearts crying, and each woman told
a second who told a third until

these moments of metaphor
took root and became
talismanic of either a sanguine
or not so sanguine future sown
in the season of weddings and rebirths
and birds building nests

A scree of crystalline blisters

(After Elaine Whittaker's art installation Spontaneous Generation, *Ablation*, 2007)

shards of homegrown salt

        surgically

    excised and placed

           in precariously hung

Petri dishes

    their shadows' glimmer

          Devon

        Ross

a harbinger

      Penny

    Ayles

of glaciers' accelerating shrinkage

    Melville

      Meighan

an adumbration of ice field

      Agassiz

Larsen B.

break-up into ice pan bric-a-brac

Ward Hunt

Filchner–Ronne

White

for the scientist explorers

white

for ablation   the totality of erosion

white   .

purged of blue

white for oblivion

and the oblivious

white for salt and salt

for the coming desiccation

for the salt crystals left

at the edge of receding seas

the salt encrusting

the lips of the thirsty

If this is elegy, how can she part with any piece of it?

The Roses Are Just Moving into Fabulosity
(Painting Sequence by Jane Martin, the Red Head Gallery, February 3–27, 2010)

Painfully, I presume, as he
parted with physical and mental vigour,
then the tumour (or some piece of it)—
a broken line on the radiation head-mask
maps the laser's itinerary—
and ultimately with life itself.

If this is elegy, what
of her remorseless portraits—face
with drooping left eye, gauze-swathed head,
and in a side-view of shaved skull,
the sutured-with-staples arc of raw scar
above a delicate conch-shaped ear.

If this is elegy,
try to gaze without flinching
at the devastated torso—colour
of slaughtered cattle,
skin sagging in folds filigreed
with blue, protuberant veins.

And dispersed among those images
paintings of pressed-glass bowls afloat
with roses from their prized garden
in fabulous and then faded bloom—
velvet red, peach, corps de ballet pink,
saffron, cerise, cerement white.

How can she part with any piece
of this pictorial chronicling of decline
and rallying and inevitable demise?
For perhaps she surmised,
after the daily photos and then the years
waited before taking up her brush,

not ownership of the finished work
but preparing the ground, mixing the colours,
drawing the imprimatura, applying the oils—these
would bring empathy and exoneration,
would become her means of surviving
the pain of survival.

Disorder and Early Sorrow

The aging professor of history sits at his desk, weary
from the burden of looking back, his exquisite task
to mute dissonances, to quiet the percussive excess
of real and rhetorical oppositions,
to discover under the cacophony a musical thread,
a coherent theme like a Wagnerian leitmotif.
His head throbs from the effort of years, his magnum opus
beginning to appear unachievable, like Casaubon's universal mythography.

As he hears drifting in through his study door
the voices of his teenage children and their exuberant friends
—all unreflectingly comfortable in the confusion of the present—
he realizes that their world is more alien to him than the courts
of Kaiser Wilhelm II or Czar Nicholas I. Even revolutions, failed
or successful, are less alarming to him, less
unsettling than the bewildering shifts and reverses
of the here and now.

Those yesterdays—a muddle, yes,
and difficult to master, but every time, given the choice,
he would choose time gone by, for at least there
he discerns some measure of *Ordnung*,
feels somewhat at home.

Compositional Essentialism

Mornings we pile into cars and drive
to an ancient hilltop town where we walk
the cobbled, steeply curving streets,
hesitantly entering the shadowed interiors
of centuries-old churches. We are startled by the fresh-
cut flowers on every altar, and by Luca Signorelli's
paintings, palimpsests of "the spiritual torment,
the deep moral restlessness of his times,"
signs of which we detect in the Madonna's down-
cast eyes and in the ardent look of Sant'Apollonia,
early church martyr who leapt into the flames
rather than renounce her faith.
But we're stumped by the figure of San Rocco,
the warrior-like sweep of his arm
commanding us to gaze at the gash in his thigh.

Evenings, back at the villa, we listen
to the male European blackbird, his versatile bursts
of competitive bel canto, inborn restlessness,
spring's mating ritual. Although we trace
his operatic peals to trees on either side of the villa,
we never catch him singing, his long pointed
black-feathered wings and yellow bill
hidden in the branches framing fields of wheat and rye,
Verdicchio vines, olive groves and rows of rosemary
that descend into the valley, fan across it, and climb
the facing hills to where, floodlit at night,
stonewalled old fortress towns lure.

Holiday

Face raised toward the sun, I lie back
in a dead man's float, the water
turquoise as a dentist's analgesic, innocent
as cellophane. Locals call this shallow,
sandy-bottomed basin "Nylon Pool."
A boatman ferried me there
through a grove of mangrove trees.
Have you ever seen one?

Thin hairless roots sprout
from leather-leafed branches, plunge
through air, splitting and arcing
like the bow legs of rickets-afflicted children,
then disappear, no ground in sight.
The scum-brown snaky tangle of the swamp,
a legendary hiding place
for fugitives and escaped slaves.

Later that afternoon, August 1,
Tobago's Emancipation Day,
I stroll the hotel beach, tracing
in bare feet a fraying rope of pebble
and debris. A dark-skinned child,
playing in the surf, looks up
and calls out after my retreating back
"Pinkie, Pinkie," no sunscreen proof
against history's sting.

Kazuo Nakamura's *Inner Structure* (1956)

Reed-thin gates to Shinto shrines or the O.K. Corral
stagger across a glowing blue field,
reel and fall, higgledy-piggledy, into piles
like dropped chopsticks. Or
spirit-possessed hydro and telephone poles
performing a frenzied dance. Or ideograms,
stripped to the bone, freed from the constraint
of syntax and calligraphic embellishment,
no longer conveying any meaning
beyond these striated cries amplified
by a turquoise blue more luminous
and jewel-like than any colour found
in nature. Or shadows from the internment camp's
towering fence, menacingly multiplied by a searchlight or,
illumined by the same roving beam, a network
of cobwebs spun by a drunken spider.

But he calls it "Inner Structure,"
so maybe we're looking
at mayhem in a mind transported
by grief or ecstasy as, in either case
neural synapses fissure, ganglia
go haywire and unravel, cross
their signals, become tangled,
collapse into obluevion.

Falling: the many kinds of

(After Betty Goodwin's *Falling Figure*, 1965)

falling

      apart
           asleep

                falling

to pieces

      falling behind

                falling

back
      away
          over
              falling through space

off a log

      the wagon,

           down the rabbit hole

falling from

      grace

           falling

dead

      the terminus

         in red

           and blue brutally

              juxtaposed

          flammable

        as acetylene

the red

           neither scarlet

       nor amaranth

          neither crimson

       nor ruby

but shrill and scratched

            a keening

         for the figure

       doubled over

    and pitching

forward

    off the edge

        into a pit piled

            with bodies

                    falling

      falling

as the red figure

        still standing

   waits

        body taut

           not yet butted

   to the ground

        for the *Genickschuss*—

           the shot

               to the nape

          of the neck—then

             falling

                    falling

            toward

                    and into

        impastoed

blue

            thick and textured

                    a blue

                not at all

        like sky

                or sea

                    or the nubby

blue towel

            his mother

                    on Saturdays

                            wrapped round his body

        to rub him

                dry

as wet and naked

he stepped

from the bath

The Foraging Gleaner

(intentional mistranslation of *"Foråret angriber"* by Niels Hav)

deaf and blind the gleaner
wears the slippers of late summer

the apple harvest beginning to fall
an offering to hospitalers and hospices

ungloved his hands rake the earth
scratching, scraping, blotching his skin with blood and soil

he stands at the unwinding of the day
fatigued amidst the traffic of loss and need

Giorgio Morandi's *Large Circular Still Life with Bottle and Three Objects* (1946)

Dating from shortly after the war,
it exemplifies his pared down and repeated
but always varied studies of pots—ordinary
vessels—pitchers, urns and jugs, decanters,
ampullae and bottle after bottle such as this one
next to a small bowl, canister with handle
and a sphere divided at its equator and ridged
like a pumpkin—commonplace objects
Morandi would dedicate the rest
of his life to, his signature obsession
already developed under Fascism,
that he was a sympathizer concealed,
post-'45, behind his image as recluse
holed up in a Bologna studio—convincing
given the nature of his still lifes, so unlike
Il Duce's bombast and posturing,
so quiet in their hazy celebration
of the utilitarian, of utensils from peasant
and worker homes, by hard necessity stripped
of all adornment, an aesthetic Morandi,
the artist, cultivated with his commitment
to simplicity and stillness, to the pottery
of the abiding, the pottery of wine
and oil and vinegar.

Fireside

Ordinarily I might see in the fire's
syncopated, fevered springing
Nolde's garish Bacchae leaping
in circles around a Dionysian Christ,
or feral tongues licking
at a *converso* sentenced to *auto-da-fé*,
but on this February evening,
snow having cut the depth of field
all day, I'm determined to resist
such sinister cogitations.
Time to lay disquieting thoughts aside,
sink into my faux leather La-Z-Boy
and enjoy the flames rising
                    like charmed snakes
from the pressed log I put a match to
when, no lamps as yet switched on,
dark leaked into the room
as from a canister of gas.

Aggrieved

Her head's a gunny sack packed with spitting, hissing feral cats, her mind a pot at-the-boil, seething with unsent complaint—letters to the editors of *The Toronto Star*, *The Globe and Mail*, *The New York Times*, *Le Devoir*, *the Guardian*, *der Spiegel*, and *die Zeit*, to the authors of disturbing poems and contemptuous reviews, to prime ministers of Canada and Great Britain, to the organizers of the Liberal Party, to the Chancellor of Germany, to the lame duck president of the United States, to the International Court for War Crimes in the Hague, and most frequently
to God.

Cracks

My mother believed deadly germs
live in cracks—particularly those gracing
diner and five & dime dishware—
insisted, to my mortification, on sending back
any food, liquid or solid, served
in a cup or on a plate marred
by the tiniest hairline fracture.

So no surprise I'm driven to ditch
the patched, the darned, the Scotch-
and duct-taped, to intercept
unsent messages, comb through books
for missing pages, suppress
aborted dreams, memories riddled
with the unresolved, for now

I, too, see menace lurking
in every fissure, extend that obsession
to the ungrammatical—the comma splice,
dangling participle, anacoluthon—
long to caulk the crevices
between floor and door, door
and frame, shudder at the split seams
in our world views, rifts in our relationships,
leaks sprung in vessels consecrated
to our holiest beliefs.

Asclepias Syriaca

To turn inward, that old temptation,
as though the mind's gathered wool
had a claim greater than prairie, than wetlands,

than this welter of tall spiky grasses,
cow bane, beardtongue, the leaves of the cup plant
like elephant ears hung from a hollow stalk.
Among patches of prairie dock and purple vetch,

I coax my mind out of its flocculent trance,
urge it to take stock of this marshy place
lying open and wild under a cloud-flocked sky
edged by black trees, scraggly, wind-twisted.

But, like those women in Victorian workhouses
coerced to spend their days picking oakum,
I keep picking at an obstinate unformed thought,
something about transience—about endangered prairie

outliving me whether or not I pay heed—
the idea fraying like seeded tufts that burst
white from the dried pod of dying milkweed.

Franz Johnston's *Where the Eagles Soar* (ca. 1920)

Even reproduced in postcard form
it sweeps the breath away—the sheerness
of the cliff, the precipitous drop. Seeing
the full-sized canvas, I feel
diminished as one is expected to feel
in the face of nature at its grandest,
its most sublime, for Johnston captures
the majesty of the wild devoid
of either human figuration or
anthropomorphic drama in roiling clouds.
How dwarfed a person would appear, I muse,
inhabiting that landscape, one
the artist himself presumably visited,
unless he spun the scene purely out of his own
imaginings, a hypothesis I doubt faced
with the work's echoing detail. As my gaze

lingers on the soaring promontory,
my awe, at first coloured by fear of venturing
onto a height where eagles soar, deepens
into dread of the vertiginous abyss.
A city girl more comfortable strolling
between skyscrapers than scaling a rock face,
I have no desire to search out the actual
ochre- and blue-tinged precipice, content
instead to sit and be daunted by a picture
on the wall of this urban art gallery
equipped with every modern convenience
and reachable by public transportation.

Late August

The last of the hibiscus flowers,
drab as the plumage of a female cardinal,
fall limp onto the warped deck. Wasps
and blue bottles scrawl graffiti on the air.
A cabbage butterfly, flapping open
and closed like a matchbook,
touches down on a rancid-yellow begonia.
Bird feeders, busy as aerodromes, sway
in a wind that stirs the leaves of the oak,
maple, willow and basswood into a rustling
like the self-important bustle of batmen
rushing into an officers' mess
with dispatches from the front, warnings
about the coming days, their
diminishing length and number.

The Long Schoolroom

I sit in my neighbourhood café
thinking back on all those years
I spent in the classroom. Some
should never teach—those
who think they don't know anything,
and those who think they know too much.
I concede that I was guilty
on both counts—depending on the subject,
depending on the day.

And the nights unable to sleep,
writhing with regret or anger or shame
or any of the other strong feelings
that held me in their vise at the end
of a teaching week. I should have been . . .
what? Ballerina, movie star,
fashion model, all unreal aspirations
of my childhood abandoned for good reason
with nothing to take their place

except doing well in school and then
continuing for decades to do well.
And at the end of more than
twenty years of schooling?
Still going to school Monday
through Friday, week after week
for the rest of my life—at least until
the golden years, according to some,
to others, the twilight years.

Sic et Non

My throat—worse
than parched—scorched.
Gullet shrunk,
cracked and curled at the edges
like charred parchment.
Forehead ice picked, skewered.

You have a true flu,
the doctor announces,
a virulent, treacherous flu—
true as in the 1918
influenza epidemic—killer
of untold millions, including Mother's
older sister Faith.

Martin Luther, believer in faith
versus works, nailed 95 theses
to Wittenberg's *Schlosskirche* door—
for disputation—thesis,
antithesis, for and against—his dialectic
more adversarial than Abélard's
Sic et Non.   Sick/

not sick—another dialectic
of warring opposites—microbial armies
locked in combat with "plenty of liquids,
plenty of rest," and the days swell
into weeks, the weeks into more than a month

as I lie in bed, drinking tea and juice,
ice water and soups while the invaders

prolong their retreat with rearguard
skirmishes until the day I wake,
alive again to the leaves of the weeping beech
deepened from copper to purple.

Kandinsky at the Guggenheim

Slowly we circle down the ramp, snaking
our way back from his last canvases
to his first breakaways (or deviations)
from *der blaue Reiter*, my friend

and I responding each in her own way
to the abstract shapes, biomorphic
and geometric, she most deeply touched when,
within the swirl, she finds a kernel

of the recognizable, triangles
suggesting firs, circles resembling bubbles
released into air, I preferring no sign
of clear text, taking pleasure instead

in the dynamism of haloed spheres
sliced by black diagonals, clash
of vibrant blue against vibrant
green, yellow, red. But strangely

we often love the same paintings,
and agree about his last works,
disliking their static flatness,
palette of pale pastels. Spiralling

down, we are reversing
time, unspooling the artist's life
from death back to birth, *Ende*
to *Anfang*, tracing a familiar path—

the day before yesterday washed out
while our earliest yesterdays blaze
bunt and *klar*—Munich and the blue
rider, blue mountain, Murnau landscape
with rainbow, locomotive, tower,
das Russen-Haus, Gabriele Münter.

Aubade

This morning I woke up
twice, first in a dream and then
in actuality, but the second felt
less real than the dreamt awakening,
the latter coruscating my mood all day
with the pewter gloom of early cinema,
the ceilings of the house in which I woke
disproportionately high,
the walls torqued, the spaces in between
diaphanous with vacancy, all power sources
aborted—water, lights, heating,
a house without sound, a shadowed silence
through which I floated to reach the front door
and, stepping out, found a ragged line
of stooped, hooded, black-mantled figures
trudging up the driveway between my house
and the house next door, their leader
gesturing wordlessly for help,
but I had none to give, so, defeated,
they trudged on, their procession
mediaeval as the flagellants' in *The Seventh Seal*,
and my friend asked me what it meant
and I replied I didn't know but guessed
a premonition of death or something apocalyptic
and now I see myself returning
in sleep to the house of my dream
and never waking up.

Unwillingness

to depart. Sound of wind
in the catalpa and eucalyptus.
The *j* of his name a soft whispered rasp.
Slices of melon in small white bowls.
The room where we lay immersed
in what would now not be.
No dog barks. No queltehue
with territorial screeching rend the air.
Outside, a chair scrapes over veranda stone.

The Last Day

I wake in darkness—*Reisefieber* the Germans call it—
to the racket of querulous queltehue, and
the competitive crow and response of roosters
one *parcela* to the next. Travel fever. Small talk
and sociability spent, it's time to go home.
As the dark recedes, I leave the villa, take the path
along the vineyard's western flank, through the eucalyptus allée,
towards the hill, Guardián at my heels. I thread my way
up the slope between spiny bushes, espy a rock to sit on
but Guardián beats me to it and showers it with piss.
I choose another. Dust-covered, yoke-yellow puffballs hang
from the unbarbed female espino like limp balloons
the morning after. I've made it up to see the sun rise one more time
from behind the Andes, a molten disc ringed in pulsing nimbi.
Is it morning mist or smog that lies in thick bands
of haze over Santiago? I gaze down at a world loosely laid out
in fields of green and brown, flowering weeds mistakable
for dandelions, the moo of a distant cow like a giant mosquito.
Still winded from the climb, I begin the descent, Guardián now
in the lead as though I don't know the way. Chicory blooms
along the canal a chalky lapis blue. What I don't know
is whether I'll ever return.

Notes

p. 11   The Kay Ryan quotation for "Visiting Neruda" comes from an interview with Kay Ryan by Grace Cavalieri in *The American Poetry Review*, July/August 2009.

p. 15   According to Nicholson Baker, "One time Roethke danced around the room saying, 'I'm the best god-damned poet in the USA!'" (*The Anthologist*, Simon & Schuster, 2009, p. 187).

p. 17   In biographies of Luisa, the Marchesa Casati Stampa di Soncino (1881–1957), she is quoted as saying of herself: "I want to be a living work of art."

p. 31   William Holman Hunt, one of the founders of the pre-Raphaelite Brotherhood, was born April 2, 1827 and died September 7, 1910.

p. 39   *After Life*, known in Japan as *Wonderful Life*, is a 1998 film by Japanese director Hirokazu Koreeda.

p. 45   The Tony Hoagland epigraph for "Dear Richard" comes from his poem "Personal," in *Unincorporated Persons in the Late Honda Dynasty* (Graywolf Press, 2010), pp. 48–49.

p. 65   "*im Angesicht des Todes*" is German for "in the face of death."

p. 85   The espino plant is a spiny bush that grows in Chile.

p. 85   The Queltehue, or Southern Lapwing, is commonly found in Chile and known for its screeching.

p. 96   *Babette's Feast* is a 1987 Danish film directed by Gabriel Axel based on a story by Isak Dinesen (Karen Blixen).

p. 97   The Robert Mazzacco epigraph is from his poem "Á Rebours," *The New Yorker*, July 11 & 18, 2005, p. 81.

p. 101   Giotto was born circa 1267 and died January 8, 1337.

p. 114   "Disorder and Early Sorrow" invokes the Thomas Mann short story of the same name.

p. 115   Luca Signorelli's dates are ca. 1445/50–1530.

p. 131   "The Long Schoolroom" takes its title from the first line of W.B. Yeats's poem "Among School Children."

p. 134   Gabriele Münther (1877–1962), together with Russian-born Wassily Kandinsky (initially her instructor, then her lover), was a key member of the Munich Expressionist movement known as The Blue Rider (*der blaue Reiter*). The house they shared in Murnau was called, by locals, the Russian House (*das Russen-Haus*).

Dedications

"Best God-Damned Poet in the USA" is in memory of Theodore Roethke (1908–1963); "Ode to David Donnell's *Sometimes a Great Notion*" is for David Donnell; "Dispute with the Old Poet" for Donald Hall; "After Life" for Dwight Raymond Boyd; "Three Rivers League" for Patricia Miklos, Mark, Emily Ann, and Clara Margaret Boyd; "In the Moment" is in memory of my Aunt Louise (1910–2009); "a grieving walk (Chile)" is for Barry Dempster; "A scree of crystalline blisters" for Elaine Whittaker; "Disorder and Early Sorrow" for Stan Dragland; "Compositional Essentialism" for Laurel Doucette, Anne Hart, James and Joan Hiller, and Kay Matthews; "Holiday" for Sherene Razack; "The Foraging Gleaner" for Stuart Ross; "*Asclepias Syriaca*" for Lindy Smith; "*Sic et Non*" for Elizabeth Greene; "Unwillingness" for Ronna Bloom; and "The Last Day" for Susan Siddeley.

Acknowledgements

My thanks to the following literary journals and anthologies for publishing some of the poems that appear in this volume, although sometimes in an altered state: *ARC, CV2, Event, The Malahat Review, Vallum, Crossing Lines: Poets Who Came to Canada in the Vietnam Era*, edited by Allan Briesmaster and Steven Michael Berzensky (Seraphim Editions, 2008), *Regreen: New Canadian Ecological Poetry*, edited by Madhur Anand and Adam Dickinson (Your Scrivener Press, 2009), and *Celebrating Poets Over 70*, edited by Marianne Vespry and Ellen Ryan (McMaster Centre For Gerontological Studies and Tower Poetry Society, 2010).

I would also like to express my heartfelt gratitude to Myna Wallin for recommending this collection and to all the people at Tightrope Books for seeing it through to publication: Halli Villegas, Shirarose Wilensky, David Bigham, and Heather Wood. At various stages in the preparation of this manuscript, I benefited greatly from the advice of three exceptional editors: Barry Dempster, cheerleader and sorcerer; Stan Dragland, the calmly punctilious; and John Reibetanz, musician of prosody. As always, I am grateful to Helen Humphreys for her long-standing support and indebted to the members of my OISE poetry group—Sue Chenette, Maureen Scott Harris, Patria Rivera and Julie Roorda—without whose encouragement, literary knowledge and laughter my life would be inestimably poorer. I should also like to thank Kelley Aitken for reigniting my interest in ekphrasis and Sue MacLeod for insightful readings of a number of poems. To the members of the Victoria University poetry group, whose ranks I have more recently joined, thanks for giving my poems such astute and supportive readings. To Ilya Brookwell, my appreciation for his invaluable computer expertise. And finally, a big hug to my partner Dwight Raymond Boyd for always being there when the going gets rough.